THE
SENSUAL
WORLD
RE-EMERGES

Eleanor Lerman

Sarabande S Books
LOUISVILLE, KENTUCKY

FIRST EDITION

Managing Editor
Sarabande Books, Inc.
2234 Dundee Road, Suite 200
Louisville, KY 40205

Library of Congress Cataloging-in-Publication Data

Lerman, Eleanor, 1952–
    The sensual world re-emerges : poems / by Eleanor Lerman.
— 1st ed.
        p. cm.
    ISBN 978-1-932511-81-9 (pbk. : alk. paper)
    I. Title.
    PS3562.E67S46 2010
    811'.54—dc22   2009021558

ISBN-13: 978-1-932511-81-9

Cover design by Kirkby Gann Tittle
Text design by Charles Casey Martin

Manufactured in Canada
This book is printed on acid-free paper.

Sarabande Books is a nonprofit literary organization.

 The Kentucky Arts Council, the state arts agency, supports
Sarabande Books with state tax dollars and federal funding from
the National Endowment for the Arts.

 This project is supported in part by an award from The National
Endowment for the Arts.

CONTENTS

The Sensual World Re-emerges

The Sensual World Re-emerges

You are on the subway, going uptown
This is the same train that your father rode,
the same city where your grandfather
made wigs in a windowless basement,
in a year so far gone it has faded into nothing
All day, you have been annoyed by
incidental problems and you are still
solving them in your mind as you drowse

In other words, you have gone over
You are not drowsing. You are asleep
But I don't blame you. So am I

When you reach your stop, you change
for another train that takes you out
to the dark suburbs, where you must
walk along a dark road. Just before
you reach the lighted street that leads
to home, from within a stand of trees

the sensual world re-emerges, in all its
naked, jackal-headed beauty, holding
the moon in its outstretched hand
But you aren't afraid: the sensual world
is an old friend. Or is it? Lately,
you have been forgetting things
and you aren't really sure

And so it stalks away, angry not
to have been embraced, leaving you
on your own, with one foot
on the shining path and
one foot closer to the pit

Call me. I have left my number
everywhere. I want to know
how this story turns out

Seven Souls

There is intrigue among the souls, and treachery.
—William S. Burroughs

What is our job? By the evidence,
you would think it is to be enslaved
For example, contrast the mysterious silence
of the natural world with your morning
melancholy, with your shopping list. In the
supermarket, your seven souls trail behind you,
angry and indecisive about the evening meal
The youngest wants to kill something
The oldest is sickly, but still hoping for
psychotropics—and these are your allies

Vicious, tired, lingering in the world
long past the fall of the final epoch
(the one that built heaven on earth and
filled the rivers with stars), they are
remnants who remember too much,
and what they remember, they whisper
to you: once, we did not have to
be conscious, and time stood still

Some say that is the primal condition,
and enviable: time stood still and I
did not know. But other forces are now
at play, which have exceeded the speed
of light, which are orbiting closer and
closer, which override the old directives

So there is no choice. The next sound
you hear will be the cracking of a million skulls
A generation of them—and dreams will pour out
At least we can hope that is how it will begin

The Body, Which Used To

The body, which used to
float down the boulevards, wraithlike,
radiating attraction, topped by
a face like a knife with a baby pout

now refuses to get out of bed.
Why? Ask it. Go on, anyone,
see what it has to say.
Are you sick? Are you tired?

The poor body shudders under its
thin sheet, each flat year laundered,
faded, gone, gone, gone.
What can it do but pull the lever

that operates a moan while the body
plunges back into sleep, into its
one dream of finding its way home
to queer street in the diamond days

when it was as brave as a boy,
as young as it would ever be, and
driving a stake into its own heart
was only a trick

Who Are We?

Who are we? You can go on for years
ignoring that question because there is
so much filing to be done—and then,
some broken day, when you're on the
long slide into a black mood, the
ancestral skull appears in a dream
Take it, the drums insist. *Jesus Christ*,
you scream, *get that thing away
from me*. And so it begins

Hubba, hubba, hubba. Now you find
that you can hear the sound of the
universe thinking about itself. If you
ask questions, it refers you to a
subclause in a subparagraph of a
page buried so far back in the manual
that no library even keeps it on the
shelves anymore. *Hubba, hubba,
hubba*, says the universe. *I am not
the boss of you, nor you of me*

Which still leaves unanswered
the question, *Who are we?* Who
am I? Who are you? All I can
figure out is that we are not who
we use to be: people who were
orderly. Who turned in our papers,

who answered the phone. We never
got paid enough but hey, in the
early days, the good drugs were
cheap. And yes, I said drugs,
not medicine, which is what
we need now. Irony, as you may
have noticed, totally abounds

So, brothers and sisters, who do
you think we are? Generations
watch the gates of heaven and hell
to see who gets paroled, but don't
expect your notice in the mail
The last guy at the last desk scribbling
the last line before his ass is fired
suggests that the walrus was as
good a guess as any. In response, the
universe boils over, manifesting a joke
about infinity by asking for more time
Apparently, there is no right or wrong
and everything that's every happened
is the result of a conspiracy. *Just as I
suspected*, says the Top Soul as it tries to
slap some sense into the Top Quark, which
will continue to charge you more than
you can ever afford, just because it can

Yours Alone

This thing—
you would think, for example, that it
would show up when you are driving
through the gas fields of a neighboring state,
the air along the edges like hair on fire,
burning up the horizon—

but that would mean it is a feeling, or a
sense memory, something that can be
experienced and then forgotten, but
it is not. It is real, or has become real—

unexpectedly. With its chattering teeth,
its anxiety that death leads to nothing—
yes, it has moved in with you and it
weeps all day. Strangely, it is
attractive to you in a way that you
did not know you found attractive:
it is thin, pale, naked, sexless—this
is what you want now? What can that
possibly mean? That you are ready to
accept that love is boundless, faceless—
even forgiving—or that you were just
going along your lonely way and this
is what happened?

Ponder all you want. The average
survival time for the disease you have
is not that long and we need your house,
your car for a more promising experiment
And take that thing with you when you go
It is yours now, yours alone

This Desire Stands Apart

There comes a time when what a person wants
cannot be contained within himself
           (herself)
This condition has been called an ache, but it
is not, although it does bear a close resemblance
to pain, as well as to what is unseen in nature
         and yet undeniably, exists
And it has intentions of its own:
it bears malice toward some, spares others,
         and for the self
can be an agony that far surpasses love
This desire stands apart—in fact, is
blind to—union with another soul because
it does not recognize the merely human as
         important
It may be better; certainly, it is *more*
It is everything that it contemptuous of
         the supernatural
It has been with you from birth and now it
         has decided not to let you sleep
Soon, it will deny you food and a place to live
         until you achieve whatever end it seeks
with such singular, devoted and passionate
yearning, of which you are the source and
         the director
How much more can you stand?
You can stand all of it, and there is no

turning back:
the horizon creates itself in the image of
your desire and counts the hours
until you cross

The Deviant

The next time I am hired
to do a job, I believe
that I will discuss
the paranormal, or
give a demonstration
of how to make candy
Not that I know anything
about these subjects,
but if you know me,
you know that has never
stopped me before

What I will not do
is push my own life
onto the stage anymore
and listen while it tries
to account for its sex,
its quality, the ballet shoes
it used to feature, the
mistaken beliefs it
clung to year after year

I could come up with
reasons: I could say,
Because it's time to leave
the poor thing alone
or, Oh, just let it

enjoy itself while
its health holds out

but if you know me
you would know
that I am lying:
at my house, what was
expected to decline
instead, is growing
stronger and the worm
that should have turned
is busy chewing its way
out the front door

And oh yes, the mind:
that machine
infuriated by mortality
That old deviant,
which has finally
decided to wake up
It thinks and thinks
and what it thinks
is beginning to seem
believable: that the
shoes were okay,
but everything else
was just ammunition

Now it thinks
it will celebrate by
spitting bullets
It thinks it will
violate infinity
It thinks what it wants
And if you know
what it wants, then
you know that it
already has a plan

The Bright City of Tomorrow

I have a long ride to my job
I get on the train in a suburb
where men and women are
determined to persevere: they
carry around two lists in their
minds, Work and Family Life
Sometimes it is a grim-death day;
sometimes the train appears to
glide through the trees toward
the bright city of tomorrow
I am not sure who sets the mood
nor can I usually remember
during the hour of travel just
what it is I have been doing
all these years, apparently with
some competency, and well
In the bright city of tomorrow,
is my position a high one, or
do I serve? And where do I
return at night? To whom? I get
the feeling that arrangements
have been made, and while I
am not unhappy with them,
the lack of clarity seems to
weigh me down. On some
sunny days I float between
appointments. At other times,

I stop at street corners and
search my life, which always
growls when I touch it. If I
knew where, if I knew when,
I would search yours, too

Incomprehensible

Summer comes with a westerly wind
The province goes green. Sometimes I
walk the rutted lane into town just to
buy chocolate. The days are mild, mild
This is the natural world, and it seems
amenable: every morning it unfolds a
blue sky, lowers the rivers so that
anyone can cross the slow, sparkling
waters. By July, you might forget
how old all this is, and that it is a ruse

There is, after all, a cold turning that
will come. The seasons transit; so do
the generations, while secret processes
go on and on—at least, that is what I
believe. Yes, it is beautiful here, yes,
I know the land, the house; the address
I will give is certainly my own. And yet,
sometimes I feel that I am already leaving
Sometimes at night there are too many
stars in the sky and voices on the radio
It is incomprehensible, what they are saying

The Sky Is a River

Here is the starting point, under a
morning moon—the worst kind:
severe and secretive, the queen of
      uncertain prospects
From out of the darkness we arrive:
units of anxiety, units of dread
Money-making units, do-gooders, idiots
Our job was to pass on our genes and
      we have done it or failed
In the meantime—or in the aftermath—
other work has been assigned. We do
      this work hour after hour
after hour. Apparently, it has no end

Here is the truth: inside us now, a light
is on or it is off and we know it,
      either way
And either way, it adds a dimension,
a realization that we are responsible
      for ourselves,
for what we do and what we believe
How can it be, then, that we have
never rebelled? Never taken back
      what was taken away?

Here is the small soul, the one
that lives behind the breastbone—

the least of all but the only one
                with eyes
It will watch you now and it will judge
That is the work it was assigned
So this is the moment when you
                will be forced to guess
who you are and where it is in time
you find yourself—perhaps guided
by nothing. Perhaps by secret things:
some say the sky is a river and the stars
at night are the lights of a great boat,
but no one knows if it is just a vessel or
                also has a purpose
No one knows why here, why now,
                why us

The Great Mysteries

Because of the dead sisters
(one apiece: a murder and a
disappearance), we have a lot
to say about religion, that old cheater,
which has grown so thin and
hollow from overuse that it is
difficult to see it anymore, even
in outline. When it speaks, it is
full of complaints, but we hardly
hear them anymore. Instead, we are
thinking about joining the Jews

The Jews are on their own and they
know it. Therefore, they are free
to explore. I understand that they
got off to a slow start (too much
dancing, marrying, baking of sweets),
but then they plunged right into
the great mysteries: it is the Jews
you will find counting souls in
the ruins, Jews buying telescopes,
Jews conferring in the library
after hours. Jews are the ones
getting older and older as they
sit in a folding chairs, in the sun
Such sadness! How hard it is to
suspect what you will never know

And yet, when a death occurs,
it is the Jews who wait outside
the door, holding hands. They feel
so bad that there is nothing more
they can do. When it was my turn,
they were the ones who put up
the Missing Person posters,
who offered a reward. Whatever
they found they brought back,
no matter how irrelevant and
then we waited together
for the evidence to mount

The Master of Suicide

Between the lazy cups of coffee and
the souvenirs, the money spent on
painted shells, we wander. You crave
cinnamon toast, I want to sleep in
the afternoon. In a cool shop on the
second floor of a house where young
boys grew into cruel men, we run
our hands through bins of silver earrings
A small voice on the radio goes clear
for just a moment, and I remember
something, but not for long
What shall we have for dinner?
How much and where and when?
Later, pretending it is an item
that you read in the paper, you
tell me that even the Master of
Suicide comes here on vacation
I ask for wine to drown my sorrows
Darling, can this be what we talked
about when we meant freedom?

Now Come the Days of Philosophy

Out of the morning—boys

Arriving with the fading stars,
in the earliest hour, barefoot,
warned by women about the risk
of running toward bad weather

but they are immortal, for now
Hurricane riders line the beach,
assessing their element. Thunder
breaks the last constellation;
the sky dogs of war fall back
Now the sea is all temptation,
sliding up the side of its steep bowl
of sand. It is there, for the boys

What does this mean to me, to you?
Not only that we may observe, but
also draw our own conclusions
Inevitably, in each action we will
seek its underlying symbol. Reckless
play has many meanings. So does
work, and love; even random thoughts

It will all come clear, or it will not
But this is the outcome, this is the place:
gone is the time for living in cities

Now come the days of philosophy, when
what we never thought to do when we
were "their age"—or did do, with all
our hearts; in fact, did better—circles back
to meet us. Here, at the edge of the world,
where boys are waiting for a great storm
to send them a wave. Little do they know

The Parable of Aging

We all have dreams at night. Even
when we think that we do not dream,
we do. And all dreams are mysterious
Sometimes they seem to say nothing
Sometimes they might as well be broadcasting
only one message, over and over again,
        directly to our inner ear

A case in point: one night, while I am in bed,
in a dream I am sitting at the counter in
a restaurant. In front of me is a cup of coffee,
a cheese sandwich on a thick white plate
It is a safe, gray day. Outside, gray clouds
are traveling between the high rafters
        of the beloved sky

And then, a person—a nonperson, really,
more imaginary than alive—walks in
holding a small animal in its arms: it may
be a little bear, a gentle panda, with tender
        little paws

There is a cloth over the animal's eyes
but the nonperson announces to the
diners at the counter that there is nothing
to feel bad about. The little bear

has been the victim of an accident:
perhaps a caustic spill, exposure to
        a toxic plume

But it will be able to see again!
Ointments have been applied and
remedies. All that will be required
now is for time to do its duty and for
        the little bear to rest

But case in point: now onward and
forever, I will be affected by this dream
To begin with, it needs little interpretation,
having spoken to me of recovery after
injury, since in a dream, small animals
often represent small children and small
children are the dream-time stand-ins
        for adults of advancing age

But this is an old lesson, one that I have
learned—as you have—more than once
So I wonder why it has been paraded
in front of me again. Literally, paraded,
since the little bear had been carried
by its handler like a package, like a delivery
        that cannot be refused

Should I expect then, that more is coming?
Probably. And now the predators, I suppose
Owls, eagles. Hungry wolves who will rip
the flannel from their faces and hiss, *No, darling,
not recovery—revelation.* Which is exactly
what I was hiding from in that restaurant
Given everything we know now, I ask you,
        wouldn't you?

Small Talk

It is a mild day in the suburbs
Windy, a little gray. If there is
sunlight, it enters through the
kitchen window and spreads
itself, thin as a napkin, beside
the coffee cup, pie on a plate

What am I describing?
I am describing a dream
in which nobody has died

These are our mothers:
your mother and mine
It is an empty day; everyone
else is gone. Our mothers
are sitting in red chairs
that look like metal hearts
and they are smoking
Your mother is wearing
sandals and a skirt. My
mother is thinking about
dinner. The bread, the meat

Later, there will be
no reason to remember
this, so remember it

now: a safe day. Time
passes into dim history

And we are their babies
sleeping in the folds of
the wind. Whatever our
chances, these are the
women. Such small talk
before life begins

No Baseball

For Philip Lerman

A dark season. Grim October, with the team
out of the playoffs. Memory releases its steel grip
and points a steel finger toward Mt. Eden Avenue,
where Daddy turns off the radio and winter descends

Static on all frequencies, for months. Gruel in our
bowls, empty wallets. The only book in the library
predicts a future in the factories. There will be
no escape from the outer boroughs, where
the laundry is pinned to the roofline, screaming
We reel it in. We beat it into submission,
which has become our substitute for sport

In the next generation, we meet again, you
and me. You mention that you have defied
the odds by making enough money to buy
a ticket to spring training. What luck!
So have I! Together, we fly away to warmer
climes. Our heart is still with the team, but
we also want to get our bearings. To do
a little shopping, have a cozy drink

Even memory relents. *Batter up*, it says,
setting Daddy free as the sun goes sailing
across the sky we love: blue, tented over
the stadium, ready to be written on
I turn to you. The players take the field

Rehoboth

If I could just rest here quietly, and
make no more impression on the
appliances. If my books could read
to me. If my work would go more easily
If I could have four more sunny days

It's such an odd business, this life
What does is consist of? A depression
summer when I laid bricks in a
garden on Charles Street, now
decades gone; a cold day in Ipswich,
looking for a writer; a beach in
Rehoboth; a dog's red bowl, his face:
I have no idea what to make of all
these memories. All I agree to is that
they are mine. Since I have written
about them here, it must be so

Did I leave out that I miss you,
whoever you are? That I don't
need your help, but I wish that you
would come and live with me
Upstairs, there are empty rooms
and the curtains move with the breezes
Someday it will be spring again
Come home, come home

The Dying Girl

The dying girl gets out of bed and comes downstairs
Her spirit makes the breakfast while she cleans the house
Don't be surprised by how hard she will work, by the
lengths she will go to make preparations; some of us
toil up to the very last minute. Some of us are happy
        no matter what

The dying girl is still human, but feels like the sky,
a great, wide, pure blueness, a wing of love shielding
the earth. She doesn't want to leave and perhaps she
won't: there is a stone box in the garden, a water wheel,
a wedding dress. Each is a piece of time she has not
spent, and each in it own way needs her. Each will
        plead her case

The dying girl may be given a reprieve—or maybe
not. It's too early to tell, too late to start all over again
Tonight, she curls up in the crook of my arm, leaving me
to stare into the mysterious face of the future with its
blood-and-fire eyes. Look, look, look: if I am strong
enough such fearsome vanity may work to my advantage
I know fire. I have walked through it, I have prayed
        to it before

So it might be a safe day for hope, for airing out
A young spring is waiting to inhabit this house
Lunch, dinner, cakes and cheese: the dying girl

is planning our meals for the mild season to come
Roses arrive. The fields bring forth their bounty
Don't be surprised: some of us fight on and on
Some cook, some dream, some wield the weapons
       of devotion

And some years are dark, all bones and steel
But then the earth turns and the golden sun grants
us an hour. We gather together, we kiss. We say
       our good-byes

Now I Walk Through This Human-Built World

I remember you on the cold streets of Montreal:
a blonde buying chocolate in a French city full
of synagogues. That was the year of the Upanishads,
when love was universal. I know that you want
to move someplace warmer now, but I have
seen you in boots and gloves, with ice glistening
in your hair. It is too late for me to change
I am here. I am content. I am still at work

Now I walk through this human-built world
with my little bag of shopping and my dreams
Light is laid like a tablecloth across the
afternoon and even the thinnest, purest saints
will eat. Quietly, people leave their offices
Quietly, they cross the square, stroll through
the park, heading home. There is nothing more
to be afraid of. I hope that you will stay with me
I am happy. Darling, even if I am lost

The City, Berobed in Blue

What do you think has come over me?
I did not feel like this yesterday
but today, all I find myself thinking is,
This could be my last apartment,
my last lover; this could be the last dog
I ever own—as if I were going to die
at any moment. Which of course
is possible (myocardial infarction,
genetic defect, lightening bolt)

The anxiety may pass, but not
the age. *Yikes,* every moment says
And then, *Look out!*

Well, what can be done but put
a good face on it? A big one,
round as a moon and glittering
to the last. Or maybe slide into
an om state, where nothing is
something and everything is
more or less of something else

Better yet, maybe it's time to think
about the city, berobed in blue,
which now appears to me in memory
as a good place for a young girl,
who only I can recognize

See how lightly she steps off into
another, and then another morning
And as if she has never done it before,
begins to breathe

Women in the Air

What is out there? Something slim and cool
An inky finger to make a print upon the
desert night: a pattern strung in stars
to prove the way is marked. Thus are you
born connected to the Great Unconscious
Look up: out of the multitudes,
among the myths and theories—you.

And what else? There are the women in
the air, the women you wanted to be like
when you were at school. Jaunty hats.
Silver wings pinned to their collars,
serving drinks on the flight to Hong Kong
Kisses on a bridge under a bough of
cherry blossoms. Look up: they are
still aloft. Thus it is possible, still,
that one of them will marry the pilot

Oh yes. I promise. Despite everything
that has happened, I promise. So look up:
remember it was to you that mama told
this story—*two doves are flying through
the air, carrying a tiny frog safely between
them on a lily's leaf.* They are The Friends
Who Would Not Be Parted, and you

have been searching for them all your life

And thus they, of course, for you

A Woman Living in a Land of Giants

There is a woman living in a land
     of giants
One day, she wakes up and says,
I have had enough of all this now,
and buys a ticket to fly away
On the plane, she drinks fruit juice
from Tahiti and thinks, *How beautiful*
     are my golden bracelets
In her heart, she feels that much has
been accomplished and who is to say
     that she is wrong?

Of course, that's just a snapshot;
it's just a guess because life tells
us nothing, except that *rules are*
rules, and *two wrongs don't make*
a right. Accepted. Now let's move on

There is a girl who feels that she is surrounded
     by too much water
Her house sits in a dry field; golden plains
     are the landscape of her country,
and yet, and yet…armed only with a spoon,
she awaits the next flood season, a vigil
     she will keep year after year
Water, water everywhere and not a drop
     to drink

You get it: she has no choice. But when
she's very old, the town will hold a celebration
   for her birthday
They will hang paper lanterns in the trees
and the lanterns will look like water lilies,
   water hyacinth

Because life tells us nothing: all it allows
is a moment of reflection—and we have
forced this. It is our contribution: a paper
lantern hangs from a tree. A band of
sympathetic giants stands on their favorite
hilltop, waving good-bye, good-bye

A Woman's Project

There were bunnies in the chalk garden
hiding under lettuce leaves. When it
began to rain, they flew away. It was
a good sign that something was up!

Soon the witches came through
the front door shaking their umbrellas
Such English manners! Each so polite,
just like a governess! That's why
we invited them: because they're
the nicest women that we know

They made the sponge cake dance!
The tea cups rattled on their little saucers
and when we read the tea leaves they
spelled out love. As if we hadn't guessed!
We were already in love: we loved
each other, everything. Magic does
that to you. So does work, in
certain seasons. So do storms

Love was our guest but became
our leader. Love spoke with
so much charm that it talked itself
into a séance. By afternoon, we'd
reached the ancients and all our
grandmothers; even our late pets

who, in the afterlife, had gained
a voice. Will the world always be
so wonderful? we asked the
dear departed. Do you still miss us?
Can you try to tell us what we
will weep for when we're gone?

And if you think you know
the answers to these questions,
then you have never learned the way
to read a fairytale, or wondered if it
really is a woman's project, witch
by witch, to crack the ice that frees
the creeks to run in springtime;
in summer, to keep the horizon
stitched safely to the shore

Perhaps it is. I am not telling. But if
you want to know, these are the clues:
there is always a house, an enchanted
garden, love telling fortunes you might
mistake for gossip, and mischief made
behind a rainstorm by like-minded women
learning secrets from their friends

Lunch Will Be Served

Just when you think that you are
on the road to success and the
medications have calmed down
your wife, plus a big sale at
the foodstore means that you
can finally buy your cat a
decent meal—that's when
you get the news that it's time
to stare calamity in the face

And what a face: it comes
at you like a speeding pie
It has three eyes. It was created
by an overdose of nuclear
radiation. Its cunning knows
no bounds. Meaning, now
you are going to pay for something
you did in a past life, or didn't
do or should have thought
about doing. If you even rated
a past life. If not, then these are
just the normal ups and downs
Which do you think is worse?

Anyway. A procession of ghosts
will carry your pencil box
down to the office from which

you will never be allowed
to retire. Lunch will be served,
but all you can expect is
a bag of blood and transfat:
In other words, to rub it in,
even the cat will get a better deal

Meanwhile, the universe remains
an incomprehensible wheel of
grave attraction. Fish, swans,
and archers lie in each other's
starry embrace while dark particles
have been driving by your house
all day in their neutrino cars,
in a hurry to do a job that will
never be revealed to us. And in
some versions of this story,
the cat has magical powers
Oh my God, you say. I had no idea

Well, now you do. In fact,
in some versions of this story,
beings of faith and light
are in the kitchen, dancing
with your wife. Then your
friends arrive, still lugging
around their own dilemmas,

hoping you will feed them
from the common pot, like
in the old days. And as tired
as you are, you think you can

Gone Are the Days of the Great Blondes

What you think is that you might
be sick. I think that I might be, too
with something that is a big disease:
estrangement, nostalgia, a condition
that waxes and wanes while you
consider what it all means. While you
wash your hair. While you make
the bed and make it again and again

Well, we have to face it: gone
are the days of the great blondes
in winter kitchens making soup,
of living in the country, of casting
spells. Of pulling roots and flowers
from the ground in the belief that only
loving hands can make the harvest

in which the world will finally change
It will not change. It is not the natural way
"The world" does not get better or worse,
it simply slides away. Blinks, forgets,
ignores all our hard work (think of the hours
in the library, studying magic) and then

enters a new phase. It feels
no responsibility to warn us that
all we can do is unburden ourselves

of the superfluous, lay down in the
fabric of everyday life and wait

For what? Picture the
unimaginable: being stalked
by a ghost with a death ray,
being saved by a Vulcan kiss

Picture tomorrow. Step out
of it. Now you are cured

Fate Is a Busy Woman

At first, when your life became a myth,
      probably you were pleased
Already a lover of laurel leaves and
lightening bolts—those young things
that accessorize any outfit—you began
to anticipate a long life, a house
      in the clouds
This, in fact, is a common mistake

The transition came abruptly, and
with a challenge: a broken bone,
a journey interrupted; fruit slices
      souring on your plate
You knew that now you were in
for some real punishment, but you
      didn't know why
That's the way they built the system:
      we never know why
It just is; it has always been
It is never going to explain itself

Of course, you could be free, but
      for that,
the one thing that you need to do,
you are not allowed to do, which is
      part of the system, too
So welcome to your role in this:

get up, move on
Fate is a busy woman: you'll only
get to see her again when you least
        expect to
In the meantime, here is some food
        and a map of
the country. Wanderer, prepare

Bandito

What gets you up in the morning?

For me it is the thought
that someday, I will be
as far away from here
as I can get

Watch me
rubbing out the lines behind me
I recommend it

I recommend
fooling everyone into thinking
that you have settled down
and then heading for the hills

The dog will bare his teeth
if instructed and meet up
with you later. It's good
you named him Bandito:
he'll watch your back

This, by the way, this is not a fantasy
It is page 69 (ha ha!) of the manual
I read when we were planning
the takeover

So it didn't happen—so what?
This is better
Wait until I tell you
what's on the next page

Nice Girls

In this decade of their lives (late, late; astonishingly,
horrifyingly late), what happens to women who were
once nice girls, and pretty enough, in an evil sort
of way, is that, realizing they have lost their ability
to attract other evil girls—or even boys—in dance
bars up and down the east coast, they begin to
think that what they ought to do is take their
meager pensions and move inland, to some hilly
town where they can rent an apartment behind
an outlet store and shut up. Otherwise, they worry
that they can't be responsible for what they might
do next—even murder is on the list. (Oh, don't
play at being shocked. I'll bet you've got a
list, too, and you're still adding names.)
Anger, jealousy: stitch them up, add a few beads
and they make a great dress to stomp around the
neighborhood in, kicking down doors, kicking
those big, puffy clouds, straight arrows, people
who are after your job, and all the years to come
that are threatening to provide only more of
the same crap. There! Don't you feel better?
Sometimes, you just have to admit that you're
not a sweetie anymore—if you ever really were
And as for that thing in the basement that you
always thought was working against you?

Well, it's older now, and ready to negotiate
Already, it's thinking of how really good
you'd look with your finger on the switch

Fasten Your Seatbelts

So you want to hear my story?
Well, I never had an accomplice;
scary as it is, I thought all this up
    by myself
Could it be that's why the older I get,
the harder it is to pay attention
    to the boss?
Blah, blah blah. I just can't listen
to a word anybody says to me
anymore except "fasten your
    seatbelts."
That I can understand

I mean, this is a nice enough factory
where I am enslaved, but all we
make is bullet-proof glass and
    little forest fawns
Personally, I've had enough
of the great, wide world hammering
at the windows and the little deer
munching grass out there in
    the bitter landscape
Maybe that's why, the older I get,
the harder it is to ride the trains
Because I feel like I can't sit
    still anymore

I feel like the future will come
        too soon

And one last thing: there was a house
I used to visit that had two yellow
        couches and a garden
When it burned down, I went
and kissed the last wall standing
        to say good-bye
Here, I thought, *this is the place*
        where I became a person
As for the little deer, I hear
they've hatched a plan to make it
        through the winter
Maybe I'll hide out with them
Remember: Einstein said that
something deeply hidden must
        be behind all this
My guess is, he didn't have a clue

Ode to Joy

Four drinks after nine o'clock at the
sports bar down by the river—the river
that is commanded by Newtonian forces,
or so they say. They also say that
particles collide, but I've never seen
that happen. And then, of course,
there is the theory that giant lizards
are patrolling outer space in spiny ships,
just waiting to gobble us up for
breakfast or else impose a system of
government that will have us all
in chains, Meanwhile, nothing fits:
have you noticed that all the shirts
in the stores are too small? Who do
they think we are? And by the way,
who are they? Why do they make
us work like this? Do you sometimes
feel that the giant lizards wouldn't be
such a bad thing if they just ate the
bad people and then stayed around
as pets? I do. I'm bored with my
current pets, those little fluffy things
I wish they had teeth like a gatecrasher
· I wish I had some influence, don't you?
I mean, who do they think they're
kidding with all this lite music and
fake healthy food? Ode to joy,

indeed—I think we're being rooked
Tune to the stations between the
stations: that's where you'll hear
what's really going on—unless
that's just another trick. (There have
been so many.) Back at the bar,
How do I get out of here? says
the human to the fully loaded
machine gun sitting three stools
away. *Transcendental meditation,*
it replies. And then can't stop laughing

I Say This Is a Restaurant

When we roll into the county, you say,
This is not a county, it's a cape
and when I ask what you mean,
you shrug. And so, as usual, I rely
on clues: in the brochures,
they say this is a vacation spot
We drove here in our car,
which is a heavy object that travels
at a variable rate of speed
Factor in that I am a safe driver
I follow all the rules

No matter, I still can't get it right:
I say this is a restaurant. You say
it is a ghost ship. Furthermore,
that may be your father out back,
the old expatriate, sitting in
his trailer with his bourbon
and his flapjacks. You know
he's dead, but you still think
he ought to serve you a meal
You really believe he owes you that

My father, on the other hand,
was a song and dance man
God, all he wanted was to be loved
Which leads me to the theory

of the few vital hours
when time is like a woman
getting on a train, and whether
she is observed or unobserved
makes all the difference
You have a different view:
you say, *Isn't it strange
how we get up every morning,
still fighting to survive?*

Which is the argument
I've heard you make when
people ask why we got married
as meanwhile, the earth's
magnetic poles reverse themselves
and tiny fires ignite around the room

Sayville

Where am I now? you wonder as you
walk along the weedy streets of the town
where the ferries leave for the summer island
There is, by the way, always such a town,
such a jumping off point, and a person
        like you alighting from a train

A person like you. Sometimes you feel that
        your house is inching away:
wood paneling and black-eyed Susans
in a pot (where is the proof that consciousness
        has ever been contained?)
Now, a cup whispers, and the view of
your yard moves slightly to the right
Everything wants to go somewhere you think
        someone once said

So where are you at this very moment?
Looking for the chair you like to sit in when
        it rains and the lights are off
Electricity in the clouds crackles with
messages, even in the off-season, when
        the ferries, supposedly,
do not make the trip across the channel

Wake up, a broom whispers, and you do,
in time to see a stranger—or just

his shoes—heading toward the dock
Sometimes, you think, there is still
    a lot to learn

Empty World, Lonely Universe

In the all-day rain there is a feeling
like ghosts will soon come walking
out of the trees. Like beyond the trees
there is nothing, nowhere, not today
and not tomorrow. This is a grim
hour in the kitchen and, you think,
unfair: sure you're going to die,
but not just yet. If it is true that
you bought this house, then you
must have been sedated. As a girl,
you would have just driven away
in a car, small, red and mean
But now that you are tethered to
no one, you should not be afraid
to take the time to weigh your
options, consult a tourist's guide
Invite the ghosts in for a sandwich
Empty world, lonely universe:
that's what they carry with them
Invisible fingers turn invisible
pages, looking for travel tips
There are none that we know of
There is just the need to go

The Days of the Week Are Explained to Me

Monday. Yes, she says, it is blue,
a lazy girl blue, pouty and regretful,
trailing a bored hand along
the windowsill in an empty room
Tuesday, we wake up late and
in a panic, rush into the office
to "buckle down," which means
both to blend in and to succeed
at any cost. Wednesday is
the mountain in the dry distance;
if we climb it we arrive at Thursday,
which is a potentiality. Plans
can be made on Thursday, next steps
mapped out. On Friday, the future
is clear and it is coming closer
hour by hour: *le weekend,* as we
used to say. In the days when those
were the kinds of things we said,
and we said them all the time

Therefore, she suggests, if we
intend to get anything done,
we must meet on Tuesday,
in a sober café, with sharpened
pencils and clean white pads
Eyes front, no meds, no drinkies

as if we are normal people
with good intentions
As if we have the kind of jobs
where we are paid with money
As if in our vicious little hearts
we really want anything to change

Zion Offers Its Condolences

Dear Ones: It's such a muggy day
Childhood weather, with just a
hint of menace, as if your parents
have suddenly disappeared

As if the great, dark house
behind you, with its witch windows,
is not inescapable as a symbol
So go right on digging your
little hole with your little

bunny shovel. Pat, pat, pat.
That is the sound of your shovel
hitting the earth. It is not hurt
but you are. You won't know it
for fifty years, but boy, you are

Because there's not one damn good
piece of business in there and
nothing's coming out. Because
though they really did love you,

those traitors, that didn't stop them
from leaving the premises. Or else
they just died—about which,
only Zion offers its condolences

Things aren't all that much
better out here in this
other universe. But still,
I send you love and kisses,
though in the standard
fashion, at the going rate

Oh, and by the way: there is no peace

A Letter to the Editor

The years are lining up to tell
their stories. I wouldn't listen
to them if I were you; in fact,
I'd send them straight back to
the battleground where they
belong, but hey, if you want
to smash things like a party girl,
go on: invite them right on in

For example, there was the year
that the phone was always ringing
in the middle of the night. It was
the looney bin (I am supposed
to say "nursing home" but hey, I'm
a little smarter than that), calling
to report that my stepmother had
run out into traffic again, waving
a knife Generally, I'd tell them
that I was not the nice one and
suggest that they call my brother
Then I went back to bed

(Actually, that last line should read:
And then I crawled back into my
paper sack, under a howling moon)

Now this is a different year and
different things have happened
For example: money is running short,
taxes are rising, and late at night, our
old friend the Sleeping Prophet wanders
through the drugstore murmuring, *No,
not this bottle. Not that bottle, either*
Perhaps it's only the fluorescent lights
that make him look untrustworthy
On the other hand, all he ever
recommends is aspirin because we're
not allowed to go near the good drugs
anymore. Imagine that. All that
practice wasted. *Om mani padme hum*

So hey, let me ask you: do you think
that this is what life is all about?
I think it should be about more
letters to the editor. For example,
I contend that if you adopt a pet,
it is honor bound to love you
(and they have those great big
saucer eyes, to boot). But now the
harder days are revving up their
engines and there are rumors
that we haven't got a prayer
What does the monster in your

closet think? Mine just went
out to rescue a greyhound,
leaving me all the time I need
to write down this complaint

At This Point, Am I Closer to Life or to Death and How Can I Tell the Difference?

(for Jean Shepherd, 1921–1999)

I guess what I am asking is,
just exactly what is important?
Because at this age, I know
and you know what's coming
next: we get The Diagnosis
and it is not going to be good

For example, think about these
bodies, these hungry constructions
that have always swanned around
as if they owned the world
More high-maintenance than
any bad-boy boyfriend, they
have been secretly plotting to
exterminate themselves since
day one, or perhaps they're
just a little dim: can't smoke,
can't read an X-ray. In the
next few years, do I have
to mention how badly
they are going to behave?

So I repeat, what is important?
Do I go to my next meeting
and make my vital points about
the future of (insert something
here that I should care about

the future of) or stand outside
the board room making angry
faces? *Am* I angry? If so,
do you have any idea just
what I should be angry about?

And how can I stop thinking about
these things? Behind Tab 3 is
information that I must review
for my next (insert something
here: report, presentation, speech)
but I'd rather be watching baseball
I'd rather be drinking. I'd rather
be dancing with my dog on a
far shore in another life where
I am smarter, more hard-hearted,
possibly immortal and armed to
the teeth. Where all I have
to do is get up every morning,
shout, *Excelsior, you fatheads!*
and then every damn one
of you (myself included)
would get out of my way

But Hey, He's Wearing a Great Costume

Bear with me, because I am going
to maintain that this is a typical day:
here we are—such sweeties!—carrying
our bag of marzipan frogs through
city streets on one of those mornings
when the sunlight feels like suds
and clean laundry, and sugar,
which comes from rich islands
where happy people live, would
          never harm us
In fact, nothing will harm us:
there is no war, no terror, disease,
death, divorce or unrequited love
Not to mention cancer
Our bones could build a bridge
Our arteries are clear glass filaments
          twinkling with stars
This morning was beautiful
It will be beautiful again tomorrow

But if this is not so, then summon
          the animals!
You tell them to their faces
(those darling faces, those
trusting eyes) about the
dark forces coming soon to
          local theaters

You tell them who screwed up
What? No more baby pandas?
No dog shows? None of
those big horses that turn
up every summer and let us
ride them around the world?

Well, maybe things will get better
At my job, the Principle of Invisibility
just showed up for work and hey,
he's wearing a great costume:
he looks like Venus and Mars
       and Kansas City.
He looks like three black girls
      with great hairdos
He looks like a smoking red guitar
In other words, we're better than
the bad guys because
we can carry a better tune

In other words, as long as
the electricity holds out,
we can still listen to the radio
Rock on, was the last instruction
that was broadcast. Or *Drive*,
he said. And hell yes, we will

We Are Lucky

Do you remember what we looked like
walking down the road to this house
with our basket of books, our pets,
trailing the glitter of our age?
You were the long-haired blonde
who knew how to light candles
I had promise. I had an antic profile
and a checkered past. We didn't even
have to arrive in order to open the door

Now there is a kind of summer
in every room. I can move the air,
which feels like linen on the skin,
and morning, noon and night
there are fireflies in the trees
outside. You think these are scenes
from my childhood, but I believe that
we are living in the here and now

Which is not so bad. Look, even
our own god says he is feeling
his age. Sometimes, all he wants is
ice cream and a baseball game
Sometimes he wants to rethink
the constellations. Sometimes he
gets angry and he doesn't know why

But he's still a friend. I don't believe
that he listens to those grim idols
wrapped up in vines who are out
for blood. Let them smoke their
cigarettes: he wants to dance
Remember? When we started
down this road he promised
we would be lucky. And we are:
nothing is going to happen today

A Rainy Night in a Crowded City

Once, I knew a man who liked to talk to me
Among the things he said was, "The problem
with writing in the first person is that you
always end up with a confessional, and sooner
or later, you're going to get sick of listening
to your own stories." This was in the era of
typewriters and pre-war apartment buildings,
but the human condition was the same
as it is now, at least in my neighborhood:
we were all selfish and preoccupied with
our own appearance (especially the length
and texture of our hair), and we spent
too much time thinking about *Who am I,
really, and what do I really want?*

And though I may have made up
that conversation, as well as placed it
in the past, you will still recognize
this list of things, few as they are,
that we were interested in back then,
besides ourselves: Celebrity divorces
Baseball scores. When the health food store
was going to get in those Hawaiian
coffee beans that we were willing to
pay extra for. How much the rent
was going to go up next year

Now here is something else he said to me,
the man I alluded to above. And he said it
in a firm voice: "The problem with trying
to gauge anything about the future by conditions
in the present, or conversely, trying to learn
anything from the past, is that we are all idiots"
He had a beard and wore glasses, this particular
man, and he drank all day. Soave Bolla
Sometimes, he kept the bottles and made them
into lamps. I don't know if it was a good idea
to drink so much and then fool around with
electricity, but if something had happened,
I imagine he would have just written it into a story,
in the first person. He was a complainer, this guy,
but at least he worked. He worked all the time

So why am I going into all this now? Because
I have a story to tell—in the first person—and
it needs some context. Here goes: Last night,
when I got on the subway, I jostled a woman holding
a copy of X. When she complained, instead of
hitting her with my shoe, which would have
once been my modus operandi, I heard myself
suggest that somebody reading such an interesting
book could have been expected to be a little more
philosophical about things that happen on a

rainy night in a crowded city. And then—though
it has taken me longer than it should have
to understand that sometimes people say one thing
and mean another—I went home, turned on my lamp,
and with an idiot's enthusiasm, began my work

ACKNOWLEDGMENTS

This book was written with the assistance of a fellowship from the National Endowment for the Arts, for which the author is grateful.

"The Dying Girl" previously appeared in *turnrow* (Fall 2007 Vol 5.2); "The Parable of Aging" previously appeared in *The Canary* (2007); "Seven Souls: (under the title "Liberation") previously appeared in *Water-Stone Review* (2007); "Small Talk," "The Deviant" and "We Are Lucky," previously appeared in *Tryst3* (2007); "But Hey, He's Wearing a Great Costume" and "A Rainy Night in a Crowded City" previously appeared in *The Lumberyard* (July 2008).

THE AUTHOR

Eleanor Lerman is a native New Yorker and unrepentant member of the Woodstock Nation. She has also been a guide in a Chinese museum, the manager of a harpsichord kit workshop, and a comedy writer. Connections between the humor of the human condition and the mysteries of infinity are the hallmark of her thirty-five-year-long writing career, for which she has received numerous awards including a National Book Award nomination, an NEA grant, and the Lenore Marshall Poetry Award from the Academy of American Poets. She is the author of four previous collections of poetry and two collections of short stories.

Jeff Tiedrich